John Greening

To Alan & Judy
and all travellers in antique lands

NEBAMUN'S TOMB

warmest wishes

John

Christmas 2015

$7/150$

Rack Press

First published in in a limited edition of 150 copies,
the first fifty numbered and signed by the author.

Author's Note:
This sequence of poems was written after visiting the British Museum to see their newly revived Egyptian collection, in particular the paintings from the tomb of an accountant called Nebamun. These remarkable works of art, dating from around 1350 BC, were 'removed' and sold to the museum by the British consul-general in Egypt, Henry Salt (1780–1827), a keen and well-placed collector of antiquities. My own interest in Egypt began rather later, between 1979 and 1981, when my wife and I were volunteer teachers in Aswan, an experience which resulted in Westerners *(Hippopotamus Press, 1982), my first collection.*

Nebamun's Tomb first appeared in The Bow-Wow Shop *(edited by Michael Glover).*

For some of the detail here, I have drawn on Richard Parkinson's invaluable guide, The Painted Tomb-Chapel of Nebamun, *published by the British Museum Press (2008).*

Published in Wales by Rack Press,
The Rack, Kinnerton, Presteigne, Powys, LD8 2PF
Tel: 01547 560 411
All orders and correspondence: rackpress@nicholasmurray.co.uk

ISBN 978-0-9931045-8-9

Printed by Artisan Print, Presteigne, Powys

I

Salt watches the saw cut a picture from his wall.
      The exquisite feathers fall from the lesser birds,
           tears of silt and straw from a hieroglyphic eye.

The Old Man sleeps in Great Russell Street and an image
        flashes. He is nowhere, somewhere on the West Bank
           or in the Underground. At Boughton House or
                buried

in a quarry near Corsham. The conservator
      lets the dancing girls go by, the wildfowl fly,
        balancing so carefully.

II

                  enough to last you
for eternity
        a thousand loaves
                a thousand portions of
                    flesh

a thousand different ornaments
              changes
of clothing
      incense
         unguent

              the saw stops
its noise
      and silence begins where that slot
ends above an owl who stares his meaning
full-face at us and goes on crying
across the food offerings, the desert pigments,
red and yellow ochre, frits of a ghostly blue

III

As in those dreams where you meet
equally with strangers and the dead you loved
that always seem to be set on a train
when they come to me, but here
follow the red lines of the tomb wall

to where the male guests are seated
like commuters from the after-life
eating a wafer, holding a handkerchief,
one with a wig, some shaven-headed,
their lotus-flowers *tssk-a-tssk*-ing

there are things you keep quiet about:
the double-flute in the mouth of the girl
who looks straight at you, the entwined
haematite of the pair behind her,
the clap that has turned into a prayer.

IV

What lay in the mud between the lute on her breast
and the rack of nine pink stoppered wine jars?

A serving man unrendered as he reached for a drink?
So some scholars think, examining a muddy elbow.

But others are sure it is the last of the women, playing
an unknown instrument, one that is redolent of

wheat and barley, date fibre, reeds, rushes,
halfa, papyrus, tamarisk, fig or flax

together with some bones and fragmented flower-heads.

V

Hard to imagine such a moment, naked girls
offering wine to both the men and to their wives,
part nightclub, part Academy Award Ceremony

where everyone has a fixed look on their face
until the prize is announced and there she goes
weeping into the lotus mic her thanks

to Henry for putting up the money, to Giovanni
for his skilful cutting and above all to...
but nobody is listening now, suppressing

their screams, they reach for the mandrake fruit.

VI

Some in baskets heaped as if they were stanza-forms,
others massed into a flock of fifty syllables,
crammed like carvings on the Rosetta Stone,
the geese are here to be inspected.

The master sits in silence.
They too keep their beaks firmly shut.
Farmers can only prostrate themselves.

It is a scribe who finds something to say
as he opens a scroll before Nebamun
and begins to recite his poem: 'The Inspection
of the Birds at the Turning of the Year'.

VII

Get a move on! he shouts
as the cows pass by. It's like
watching paint dry. *And don't
talk, talking is what he hates!*

VIII

A fragment – why did this survive? – shows the barley
unharvested and upright with an old man bent over it
speaking to his own hand. As if an entire existence
had decomposed around him, yet he is fixed on this
augury in the lines of his palm. Over his shoulder
the grey mud-plaster encroaches like the North Sea towards
the cliffs at Dunwich. And above his earth-colour
a hieroglyphic armageddon hails on to his bald patch's
frizzy halo. Across the field from him the chariots
are ready to rumble off to war once the master returns,
who has leapt down to inspect the yields and convert them
into armaments. He has left his horse in the clutch
of a slave who can barely restrain its dark grey
from bolting out of the picture, having seen what's next.

IX

i bring you a hare
which i hold by the ears

it stares indignantly yet
knows it has the final

word   not only its fine
coat of yellow and white

with red speckling stripes
and black bristles   not only

its pink inner ears
and perfect whiskers   but that

the hare in hieroglyphics
means to exist

X

Let the empire spin
at the centre of this lunging
after birds that are so plentiful
nobody dreams of a time
when there is conservation. They fly
away into nothingness
to the swish of nets and stones
and guns and passages collapsing.
The fish too – mullet
and a fat puffer so pleased
with its poisonous self to be
on this white peninsula – sink.
A single butterfly is heading
for the hunter's toes and soon
African Queen, as it is known,
or Plain Tiger, will pass
into amnesia. Though there are
other humans, though there is
a goose that stretches optimistically
from the prow as the raised arm
swings against wagtail and wheatear
and shrike, it is the cat
carries the day, devouring
her soliloquy with a mouthful
of wing, her gold leaf eye
on the future, who will strike.

XI

There is a garden in the next world
where all the birds and fish and plants
that we have exterminated are being kept –

I think it is this seedbank that I visit
occasionally when I am sleeping and wake
to feel as if some part of me has gone out

and spent the night travelling, as Egyptians
used to believe and so would leave a false
door out of their tombs. Within that garden

which I imagine to be like the one at Kew
where my parents lived and where I was born
and taken through the penny turnstile

and in which there is no perspective, fish and ducks
lying sideways against the surface of the pool,
trees unfolded flat from its edges, yet where all

comes into a true angle because the light
is the light that was in Egypt when we were there,
the fragmentation of the tomb will hardly matter.

This will be enough: just as a speck of DNA
can reconstruct the scene, the life, I am hoping
that in this garden there is somewhere that I can learn

to plant and grow things as I never let myself
be taught by my father or to pave a proper path
as I watched my mother do. There will be fruits there –

I can see them in this last surviving scene, the dates,
the figs, the ghastly dom. But also grapes. And some papyrus
for writing on too, if in that garden writing is allowed.